Changing the game

for teens

GWEN GODMAN
Illustrations by Matt Glover

Published by Equip Counselling & Consulting
Bully Resilience – Changing the Game: Teen Guide
www.equipcc.com.au
ISBN: 978-0-6483687-1-7
2019
Written by © Gwen Godman
Illustrations by © Matt Glover
www.mattglover.com
Cover & Layout Design by Cara King
Edited by Daniel Godman

Other books in the series:
Bully Resilience – Changing the Game: A Parent's Guide
ISBN: 978-0-9953613-9-3
2017

CONTENTS

CHAPTER ONE:
An old problem 5
This book is for you 6
You always have a choice 10

CHAPTER TWO:
Resilience 11

CHAPTER THREE:
The Bully-game.............................13
Bob and Ollie................................14
The Bully-game is a game of power............15

CHAPTER FOUR:
The Game Players..........................17
The role of the bully in the Bully-game 17
The role of the victim in the Bully-game ...19
You are not a victim 20

CHAPTER FIVE:
What keeps people in the game?..............21
The Behaviour Burger 21
The A.B.C Burger 22
What happens in the Bully-game 24
Ollie's A.B.C. in the Bully-Game 25

CHAPTER SIX:
Repetitive Teasing Topics 27

CHAPTER SEVEN:
Changing the Game 30
Be Prepared.................................31
STRATEGY ONE:
The Line of Separation 33
STRATEGY TWO:
Do Not React 36
Reacting Vs Responding 37
STRATEGY THREE:
Switch off unhelpful social media..............40
Is it helpful?.................................40
Topics change quickly..................41
STRATEGY FOUR:
Find Your Voice............................43
What does it mean to 'find your voice'? ...43
Say what needs to be said 44
STRATEGY FIVE:
Engage Support............................46

CHAPTER EIGHT:
Wrapping it up 48
Be a team 48
Remember the ABC Burger.........................49
The journey to resilience is on-going..........50

 1. The Line of Separation

 2. Do Not React

 3. Switch Off Unhelpful Social Media

 4. Find Your Voice

 5. Engage Support

CHAPTER ONE:

An Old Problem

Bullying is a problem that has been around for a very, very long time. It is also a problem that will continue to exist long into the future. Despite all of the programs and books intended to help stop bullying, it still happens!

I have experienced being bullied. My kids have been bullied and my parents were bullied – that is just one family. Imagine that same pattern being repeated over and over for every family there has ever been. That is a lot of people being bullied and a lot of people doing the bullying. Have you got the picture? It is a nasty business and it is not going to stop.

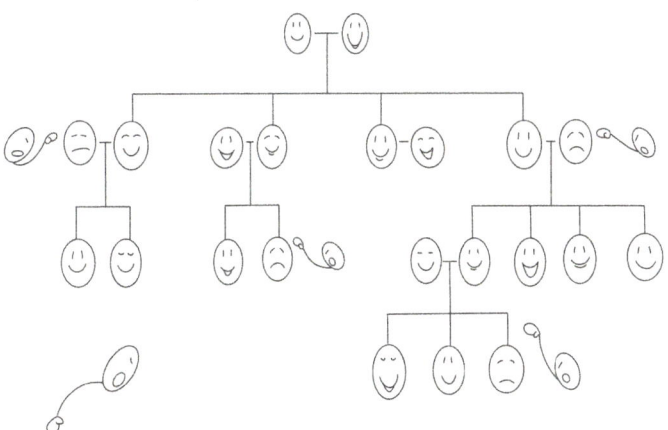

Bullying keeps happening one generation after another

This book is for you

If you find yourself getting upset because of teasing, taunting or bullying, then this book is for you. Perhaps you feel as though you cannot help it. Maybe you have been teased until you are angry and crying. Perhaps you feel miserable because it feels like people are always being mean to you. Please keep reading to learn what you can do to change this.

Your reactions may be:

1. Clenching your teeth quietly. 2. Feeling annoyed or hurt and not showing it. 3. Yelling and screaming. 4. Crying in front of others. 5. Hiding to avoid other people. 6. Kicking or punching.

How do you react to bullying?

Reactions can be so automatic that they are like a computer's default setting. But what if you could change the setting? What if you could cancel your automatic reaction and have choice instead?

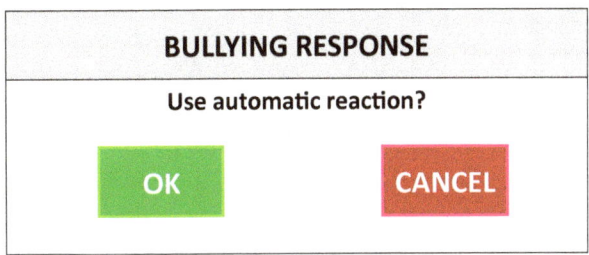

My message to you is that *you have a choice* in how you respond to being bullied. You always have a choice. It *is* possible to stop other people from having power over your Mind and Emotions. It requires making some helpful choices.

If there has been physical bullying, then please tell a trusted adult.

This book is your helper

Have you ever tried the Dodgem Cars at festivals and carnivals? I have enjoyed zooming around on them, and I have enjoyed watching others. For those who keep crashing, the ride attendant usually stands on the back of their car and will take temporary control of the steering wheel. After receiving some help, the driver continues on with more success.

With this picture in mind, I would like you to consider this book as being like the attendant on the back of your dodgem car. With a bit of guidance, you'll be able to steer yourself through life, instead of getting knocked around by others.

It's time to get some help

This book aims to introduce you to ideas and strategies that will help keep you safe. How you feel does not need to depend on how others treat you.

How you feel should not depend on how others treat you

Being **Bully Resilient** is about being able to feel calm and being able to protect your Mind and Emotions. Just like water runs off the back of a duck, being **Bully Resilient** means that hurtful words do not stick.

Bully Resilience means insults are like water off a duck's back

Unfortunately, some people have experienced a lot of bullying for a very long time. If you have suffered from this type of bullying then you may need some extra help to feel good about yourself and to learn how to feel safe. *There is no shame in seeking help.* Unfortunately, if you have a history of being bullied, it is easy to feel like you are a target for bullies.

Some people feel like a target for bullies

You always have a choice

The Number One Goal of *Bully Resilience*: changing the game, is to teach you that you have a choice.

A bullying incident occurred when I was about ten years old and I went to a friend's house to play. My friend had other friends over and one of them started to tease me by calling me names. I remember reacting with, 'I am not!' Another joined, and then my friend joined them in teasing me. It was horrible. I only knew of one way of reacting and that was to continually say 'I am not', and 'stop it'. I was outnumbered. The more I reacted, the more they teased me.

As an adult, I have wondered why I stayed there. They were clearly not going to stop. I was also free to leave whenever I wanted to, but I didn't. I stayed even though I was upset and embarrassed.

I have concluded that I DID NOT KNOW I HAD A CHOICE. I only knew how to continually defend and react, even though it didn't change anything. I had a choice in how to respond but I didn't know it. The ability to choose is empowering.

You always have a choice.

As you read this book, I invite you to:

- think differently about bullying
- think differently about bullies
- think differently about yourself.

This book will also introduce you to strategies that will help you break free from being controlled by other people.

CHAPTER TWO:

Resilience

Resilience is the ability to bounce back. We may refer to a person as being resilient when, despite difficulties and set-backs, they don't give up but keep on going. Their desire to keep going is stronger than the difficulties they have experienced. Similar words are: grit, inner-strength, determination and tenacity.

Imagine grabbing a jacket out of the cupboard and as you put your hand in the pocket you find $50. You have had this money all along, but you didn't know it. Resilience is a little like that. It's always been there but you haven't learnt how to access it.

Finding a resource that you didn't know you had

Resilience is about making helpful choices. Like the money in the pocket that you didn't know about, it is possible that you have been unaware of the choices that are available to you. One of the reasons why we are unaware of our choices is because we may think our automatic reaction is the only way to respond.

Resilience is an empowering choice. I have a distinct memory of the day I deliberately decided that I would not let a particular person hurt me anymore. I was about 13 or 14 at the time and my attitude toward them completely changed. I stopped being afraid of them and I was proud of myself for not letting them have power over me. Choice is empowering.

Resilience results from enduring the tough stuff. The development of resilience requires challenges. There may still be tears and upsets and times when you want to give up. However, by pressing on, your resilience will become stronger and the day will come when you make a resilient choice automatically. You might even surprise yourself with how calm you felt in a difficult situation. It is certainly a time when you can give yourself a high-five.

Give yourself a high-five

Resilience can be shared. When my resilience is low, or is stretched thin, I turn to a family member or friend. Their words of encouragement and guidance really help me. It is like I am borrowing their resilience for a while. You might need to ask someone you trust for some encouragement and help.

CHAPTER THREE:

The Bully-game

Like all games, the Bully-game has conditions or rules. The Bully-game conditions are a Tease followed by a Reaction. This is often referred to as the tease/reaction cycle, because it just goes on and on, and around and around.

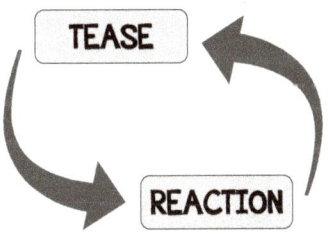

The tease/reaction cycle

By thinking about bullying as a game that is played, and by understanding how that game works, you will be in a better position to make choices. This book will show you how the Bully-game works AND what you can do about it. Being stuck in the Bully-game is disempowering, upsetting, and can be very distressing. I will introduce you to a New-game, a game that will be *Your Game* where you make the rules. In this New-game, there is no tease/reaction cycle.

> *The New-game is explained in chapter seven.*
> *Feel free to jump ahead and have a look.*

Bullying is an unfortunate part of life and it does not stop once you become an adult. The negative effects of childhood and teenage bullying can stay with you long in to your adult life. Bullying doesn't stop after secondary school ends. It is something that you will continue to encounter. This is why it is important to be *Bully Resilient*.

This book will help you recognise the Bully-game and help you understand why it is *so easy* to get caught in it. You may have been told many times not to react to bullies, but then you get bullied and you react anyway. This book will help you to explore why that happens.

Bob and Ollie

Bob the bully cat   *Ollie the timid cat*

The characters of Bob (on the left), and Ollie (on the right) will be used to explain the Bully-game, and the roles played by those in the game.

The original Bob and Ollie were quite different - they were my pets Bob the dog and Ollie the cat. Bob consistently played the Dog-pack-game, and Ollie played the Cat-princess-game. Bob would nip at Ollie and push in front of her to get attention. As far as Bob was concerned, the Dog-pack-game meant that Ollie needed to be kept at the bottom of the pack. However, Princess Ollie gave no regard to Bob and her indifference kept her safe from the Dog-pack-game. Transfer this idea to the Bully-game and your choice to play your own New-game. By playing your own New-game, you will have the power to stop the tease/reaction cycle of the Bully-game.

The Bully-game is a game of power

The Bully-game is where one gains a sense of elevation by pushing another down. Imagine two people who are the same height, and one of them is in a hole; with one person in a hole, the other now appears taller. This is what happens with bullying: the bully looks and feels elevated because they have pushed the other person down.

Bullying pushes people down

The goal of the Bully-game is to create a power imbalance where one exerts power over another. The one reacting knows that bullying is wrong and should not happen. Of course it shouldn't happen – but it does. This is why you need to learn how to be *Bully Resilient*. Bullying is not going to go away.

To help highlight what takes place in the Bully-game, I have created an acronym from the word **GAME**:

G.A.M.E. Gaining **A**ccess to **M**ind and **E**motions.

You react to bullying when it has **G**ained **A**ccess to your **M**ind and **E**motions. *Bully Resilience* is about protecting your Mind and your Emotions.

CHAPTER FOUR:

The Game Players

Now we know the game, it is time to learn about the roles played in the game.

The role of the bully in the Bully-game

Bob the bully in the game

Bob the Bully Cat represents the one who is in the role of The Bully. Being a bully is not who Bob is. Bob has his own personal story as to why he is caught up in the Bully-game.

Bob plays his role by teasing and taunting and he might actually treat everybody the same, it's just that Ollie reacts to him. When we consider the role that Bob is playing, we will see that Ollie's reactions are not helping.

In the role of the bully, Bob is:

- *not* interested in trying to understand Ollie
- *not* wanting to be proven wrong
- *wanting* Ollie to react

The one who bullies is not wanting to be proven wrong

Now that we know this, it reveals how pointless it is for Ollie to react and defend himself.

Is it fair? NO!

Is it right? NO!

Will it continue to happen? YES.

The role of the victim in the Bully-game

Ollie, playing in the role of victim in the Bully-game

Ollie is our focus and is the unwilling player of the Bully-game. Ollie might be referred to as The Victim of the game, but being a victim is not who he is.

There are two roles happening for Ollie; there is what he thinks he is doing, and what he is really doing.

What Ollie *thinks* he is doing	What Ollie is *really* doing
Defending himself	Giving Bob what Bob wants
Resisting the taunts and teasing	Inviting more taunts and teasing
Showing that he should not be bullied	Confirming that he is the one to bully

Bob and Ollie are both keeping the Bully-game going. Even when Ollie goes quiet and withdraws, it is still a reaction because his behaviour has changed as a result of Bob's teasing.

You are not a victim

Your life and sense of wellbeing should not depend on the unkind behaviour of others. Maybe you have never known any other way to respond. But you have resilience within you. Like the money in the pocket, you have been unaware of your resilience and unaware of the choices that are available to you.

Being a victim of bullying does not make you weak, helpless, pathetic or a loser. You are simply caught in an unfair game.

CHAPTER FIVE:

What keeps people in the game?

If the Bully-game is such a bad game, then why do people keep playing? What keeps people behaving in ways that are unhelpful? The word 'behaviour' means anything that a person may do. This includes things that can be seen like talking and walking, and things that may be unseen by others like feeling sad and worrying. Behaviour does not happen by itself; something happens before a behaviour and something happens after it.

To help explain how 'behaviour' works, I am going to use the illustration of a burger. A burger consists of three main parts: the bun on the top, the filling in the middle, and the bun on the bottom. The filling in the middle needs the bun to make it a burger.

The Behaviour Burger

What happens before and after a behaviour can have strong influences on what the behaviour will be. For example, when it comes to a hobby, you know you enjoy your hobby and want to do it (what comes before), you do the hobby (what you do), you had fun – so you'll do it again (what happens after encourages you to do it again).

The words used to describe this process are:

- **A** is for **Activator** – what goes before a behaviour
- **B** is for **Behaviour** – something that you do
- **C** is for **Consequence** – the result of the behaviour.

The A.B.C Burger

This ABC technique is used to train pets to do what we want them to do, and to discourage them from what we don't want them to do.

For example:

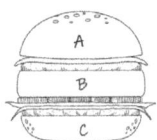

A. We tell the dog to sit (the Activator)

B. The dog sits (the Behaviour)

C. The dog's behaviour of sitting is rewarded with a treat (the positive Consequence increases the likelihood of the dog doing it again).

Now that the dog knows about the treat, **another ABC begins**.

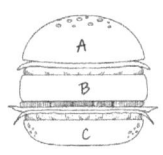

A. The dog wants a treat (the dog's Activator)

B. The dog sits when he is asked to (the dog's Behaviour)

C. The dog is rewarded (the dog's Consequence).

Notice how the dog owns all of it; it is the *dog's* Activator, the *dog's* Behaviour, and the *dog's* consequence.

The dog wants a treat – this is the Activator

This second lot of ABCs starts with the dog wanting a treat. The dog owns the *Activator* which is his desire for a treat. The command to sit isn't going the change the fact that the dog wants a treat.

This is not a new idea. Did you get stickers or pocket money for doing chores? That was the ABC model being used.

What happens in the Bully-game

It is my suggestion that the reason you react to bullying is because the bully teases about a hurtful topic. Maybe they called you stupid and you don't want to be stupid (regardless of your intellect), or they called you fat and you don't want to be fat (regardless of your body size).

One of the reasons we react is because we don't want what the bully says to be true. It is as though the bully is confirming one of our worst fears. This fear (of being stupid, fat, idiot, loser) becomes our Activator to our reaction (our Behaviour). Have a look at what it looks like with Ollie.

Ollie's ABC in the Bully-game

Ollie's Activator

When Ollie reacts to bullying, the Activator is *not* Bob, but what Ollie *fears* Bob is saying about him. Bob's tease *triggers* what Ollie fears. If Ollie fears that he is unlikable (or fat or stupid) then he reacts to Bob's teasing about these topics. It is as though the tease has the power to make it true. If he didn't care about it, then he wouldn't react.

Ollie's thoughts are his Activator

Ollie's Behaviour

When Ollie reacts, he might cry, or get upset, withdraw and go quiet or pretend that he is not upset and then get upset and angry at home.

Ollie's reaction is his Behaviour

Ollie's Consequence

Ollie wants Bob to stop teasing him, *but it is not the consequence that he is getting*. Instead, the Bully-game continues and Ollie is more miserable and more worried about being teased (Ollie's Activator).

Ollie's Consequence is that the Bully-game continues.

CHAPTER SIX:

Repetitive Teasing Topics

Bob has a predictable list of teases

While there is nothing nice about teasing, there is also nothing new about it. Teasing has been around for such a long time, that the teasing topics just go around and around; the words might change, but the topics remain the same.

The common topics of teasing include:

- intelligence – name calling such as stupid, dummy, idiot, nerd

- body shape – calling a person fat, skinny, short, tall

- body features – criticising personal features such as nose, legs, eyes, a need for glasses, hair colour

- athleticism – making fun of someone due to how they run, kick a ball, play a game

- race and ethnicity – teasing connected to skin colour or family's culture
- homophobic insult – calling people gay regardless of their sexuality
- sexuality – making fun of any who identify as either gay, lesbian, bisexual, asexual or other
- gender inequality – boys putting girls down, girls putting boys down
- gender expression – boys being called a girl, girls being called 'butch', boys being told to 'man-up'
- sexual expression – describing someone as frigid, slut, easy

These topics suffer a painful amount of repetition. Of course, there are other topics such as hygiene, taste in music and clothing. All of these topics are used in an attempt to demonstrate to others that you are different and somehow less-than, and that you deserve to be teased about it. The common element with these topics is that *they are all personal*.

When someone makes fun of something personal, it can trigger the way you may already judge yourself. This is your Activator. A tease can feed a belief that you are somehow wrong, broken, flawed and therefore, not 'normal'. These personal topics can result in strong feelings of self-consciousness, embarrassment and shame.

Personal teasing can trigger embarrassment and shame

Shame is an uncomfortable emotion that suggests that there is something deeply wrong with you. This is also when your brain is now being the bully by telling you unkind stories about yourself (everybody's brains do that). This is when you need to be your own best-friend and treat yourself with kindness. This is about reducing the strength of the thoughts that served as the Activator to the tease.

It is my experience that those who do not react to teasing and personal insults are also comfortable with who they are. They're ok with being 'different' and really do not care what anybody may have to say about that. Teasing and insults carry no threat.

I recently heard a parent complain that her son had been called 'weird' and he was now too embarrassed to go to school. I was quite surprised that 'you're weird', had become such a powerful and hurtful insult. Personally, I cannot tell you how many times I have been called 'weird'. In fact, I think I would be quite disappointed if instead of telling me that I was weird, I was told that I was just like everybody else.

Weird and proud

Demonstrating that you are not threatened by teasing remarks and cutting put-downs makes the tease powerless. Feeling threatened, offended, upset, and reacting, is part of the Bully-game. You need to change the game to protect your Mind and Emotions by making the deliberate decision that you will not let it have power over you.

CHAPTER SEVEN:

Changing the Game

Ollie needs to protect himself, but stopping Bob from bullying him is not something that he can control. However, with the help of some strategies and a different game, Ollie will be able to stop Bob from Gaining Access to his Mind and Emotions. In the Bully-game, Ollie's reactions are causing him to be more vulnerable to future attacks. Ollie needs a New-game.

> **We have no control over another person.**
> **We only have control over ourselves.**

The New-game provides an opportunity for Ollie to protect himself. If the New-game also ends the bullying, then that will be a bonus. In the New-game Ollie's behaviour will be different. In the New-game, Ollie will have the choice not to react to Bob. Like my cat Ollie and her Princess-game, cartoon Ollie will be playing a different game to Bob.

Be Prepared

Changing the game is about <u>being prepared</u>, and <u>sticking to your plan</u>.

<u>Being Prepared</u>: Your decision about how you will respond is made before you get to where the bully might be. You might even rehearse your new responses with a parent or a friend.

<u>Sticking to your plan</u>: Remain determined to not react to teasing comments or manipulative accusations. The bully may try to suck you back into the Bully-game. Be prepared, it might get worse before it gets better.

Refuse to be at the mercy of what another person may say. Put a new way of behaving into practice. You may not be convinced of your own strength to do this, but stick to your new plan. Your strength to resist the Bully-game will grow as you learn to protect yourself. Your aim is to stop the tease/reaction cycle. You have no power to stop the tease, but you can stop the reaction.

Your connection to your resilience will gradually build. The wonderful thing about connecting with your resilience is that it gets stronger with use.

Ollie is ready for his New-game

Your New-game includes the following strategies:

> **Strategy One** – The line of separation
>
> **Strategy Two** – Do not react
>
> **Strategy Three** – Switch off unhelpful social media
>
> **Strategy Four** – Find your voice
>
> **Strategy Five** – Engage support

In your **New-game**, you will be choosing to protect yourself by choosing not to play the Bully-game. You will be choosing to respond differently. In the New-game you can prevent the bully from **G**aining **A**ccess to your **M**ind and **E**motions.

Now it's your turn

To help the process, I encourage you to give your own New-game a title. What if you called it the, 'You-cannot-upset-me-game,' or 'I'm-awesome-and-you-can't-change-that-game.' My game has a simple title, it is called, 'I-do-not-play-other-people's-games.' This title has served me well.

What will your game be called?

STRATEGY ONE:

The Line of Separation

Ollie draws a line and separates himself from Bob

This strategy requires some imagination. Ollie imagines a line between him and Bob. This line creates a sense of separation and distance from Bob.

With his imagined line:

- Bob is on one side of the line and Ollie is on the other
- What Bob says and does stays on his side of the line
- Ollie's side remains a bully-free-zone
- Ollie is able to become more *Bully Resilient*.

This is a boundary to keep him safe. Ollie works hard at this new strategy and has to keep reminding himself of the line.

Of course, for Ollie to be super safe from Bob, he would need to be in a different location to Bob. However, there may be times when they are in the same space, so Ollie creates some distance in his mind. Ollie has a choice whether he listens to Bob or not.

This strategy can require some determined self-talk and imagination. It's ok if you have to chant in your mind, '*I am on my side of the line, and they are on their side of the line*', '*Everything they say and do stays on their side of the line*'.

The more you use this strategy, the easier it gets. I know of some who imagine rings or coloured bubbles around people.

Bob and his words stay separate from Ollie

Now it's your turn

Draw a picture of the people who are playing the Bully-game (stick figures work well), and draw circles around each of them. If it helps, write some of their words in the bubbles with them. This activity helps you to see what others do or say 'belongs' to them, it stays in their bubble with them.

STRATEGY TWO:

Do Not React

Ollie does not react to Bob

The second strategy of not reacting, is more possible when your line is firmly set in place. Not reacting also brings a direct change to the conditions of the Bully-game. Without a reaction, the tease/reaction cycle stops and so does the Bully-game. It would be like someone trying to play table-tennis with you and you are refusing to hit the ball back. It just doesn't work.

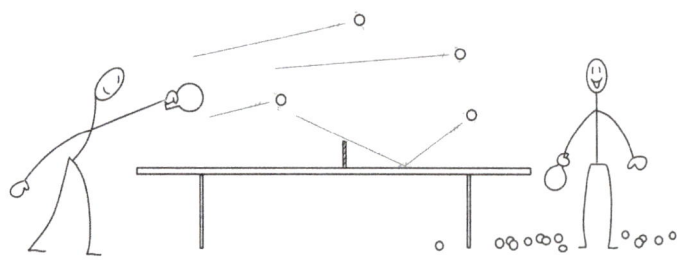

Not reacting is like not hitting the ball back

Reacting Vs Responding

The 'reaction' in the Bully-game refers to the provoked reaction that pushes back in order to defend or retaliate. The goal of the reaction is for the bullying to stop – but it doesn't stop. It might be a reaction that is emotional: sad, an angry outburst of insults, crying or perhaps you might withdraw or you might have reacted physically by hitting or kicking.

Reacting to the bully doesn't solve the problem

People have been keen to tell me stories of when they stood up to a bully and the bullying stopped. These occasions do happen but it is not something that I encourage. People who bully can become incredibly mean, malicious and manipulative when another attempts to out-bully them. That is how the Bully- game works (it's like the dog-pack-game).

'Responding' is when you are not ignoring the person but you are not trying to defend or get back at them either:

- You might agree with them; '*Yes, you are right, I am overweight*'
- You might respond neutrally, '*Whatever*'
- You might seek to be indifferent, '*You can say that if you want to, I really don't care*'.

Ollie maintains his own sense of power by choosing not to react to taunts and teasing. He is now playing his own New-game where he chooses not to get upset by what Bob says or does. Ollie decides this before he encounters Bob. Ollie's New-game establishes boundaries that protect him. Hurtful comments are recognised as unhelpful and are not worth giving attention to.

Ollie knows that:

- Bob wants a reaction
- Bob is not interested in knowing Ollie
- Bob is not looking to be shown that he is wrong.

Bob: Hey Ollie, you're so stupid.

Ollie: That's your opinion (*Ollie doesn't add anything else to it*).

Bob: Yeah well, it is my opinion, and I think you are an idiot too.

Ollie: (*shrugs and remains straight faced*) Whatever! (*Ollie walks away*).

Responding without getting caught in the Bully-game

Ollie is starting to feel more in control of the situation. Even though Bob has been insulting, Ollie has realised that there is nothing that he can do to change Bob. He concentrates on his own behaviour. Ollie responds with, 'Whatever' and walks away, and didn't react to what Bob said. The tease/reaction cycle has stopped.

Ollie is learning that people being mean and thoughtless is part of life. He is also learning to stop hurtful words from Gaining Access to his Mind and Emotions. Ollie has no control over Bob. Bob's behaviour is Bob's and Ollie's behaviour is Ollie's.

Ollie knows that if Bob was to physically harm him, then he would need to tell his teacher and his parents.

Now it's your turn

What will your New-game look like? List some possible responses that do not play into the Bully-game.

STRATEGY THREE:

Switch off Unhelpful Social Media

Ollie switches off unhelpful social media

Social media certainly has its benefits, but it is also the cause of much heartache. We all need to be cautious with how we use the internet. Conversations are had in real time and posts are shared globally. Pictures can be exchanged and passed on with little thought as to where they may end up and how many people may see them. Connectedness has never been so practiced and so expected, even homework is done online.

Is it helpful?

Ollie gets home from school and Bob draws him into an unkind or inappropriate online conversation. Sometimes it involves others and sometimes it is just Bob and Ollie. Ollie has the choice of participating in the conversation or not. If the conversation becomes negative or unkind, **Ollie needs to ask one simple question,** '*Will it be helpful?*' Does he want Bob to be reaching into his safe space of home?

Ollie can do one of two things; he can either shut down the program, or he can change his settings so that he appears 'offline' to Bob. Whichever he chooses to do, he is making a choice that is helpful for him. This is where his power is in this situation. If he has switched it off, he can now push himself away from the computer, have a stretch and go do something else. Ollie has exercised his ability to make a deliberate decision that has kept himself safe.

The strategy of walking away (also useful when you are physically facing your bully) is one of power. However, be aware that bullies don't like this and may try harder to draw you back in.

Topics change quickly

If you are feeling particularly hurt, vulnerable or threatened by a current story about you circulating on Social Media, then be prepared to wait it out: Stay safe, surround yourself with those who care for you and wait for the dust to settle. At the time, these things can be all consuming, overwhelming, and humiliating. However, topics move quickly. If you are 'the hot topic now', you won't stay the topic for long. People get bored quickly and topics of today soon become topics of yesterday. The topics of social gossip soon change to the next topic that grabs people's attention.

Hurtful discussions and arguments via text messaging and other forms of instant messenger is a phenomenon that has crept into our culture. In these exchanges, people can be far more abusive and nastier than they would be face to face. Another problem that arises is when someone makes hurtful comments in the evening and then at school they behave as though nothing has happened.

Gone are the days when going home meant having a break from school with conversations and interactions now following you home. You need to guard yourself against potential harmful conversations and comments. The urge to keep looking and watching and interacting can be strong, but again I remind you, the decision to stay connected or to walk away is yours. Cyber bullying is a problem and there are many resources available that address it in comprehensive detail.

Now it's your turn

Decide what your personal boundary will be so you will know when it is time to switch off. What topics and comments will you regard as inappropriate and off-limits? Make a list of the kinds of interactions that you regard as crossing your boundary.

STRATEGY FOUR:

Find Your Voice

Ollie finds his voice which has been there all along

Up until now, Ollie has had difficulty expressing himself to Bob in ways that have been helpful. Ollie needs to find his voice to say what he needs to say without him being dependent on the outcome of this conversation.

What does it mean to 'find your voice'?

The concept of 'finding your voice' can be difficult to understand. This is more than just having the ability to speak. This strategy is about stating what you need to say to protect yourself and to establish boundaries. This strategy can be quite challenging, so practicing what you need to say can help. Write it down and read it out loud, '*I want you to stop teasing me.*' It is stated as a fact. If the other person doesn't comply, then move on – don't get sucked back into the Bully-game.

This strategy is about learning to speak up when in the past you may have kept silent. If Ollie is not used to saying what is on his mind, then this may be a new skill for him to learn. Ollie may need to develop his ability to use his voice at home or with a trusted friend.

Say what needs to be said

In the Bully-game, Ollie *needed* Bob to stop teasing him because Bob's teasing was making him feel bad. In the New-game, how Ollie feels is not dependent on what Bob may say or do. Ollie tells Bob to stop teasing him for the purpose of letting Bob know that he has a boundary. Ollie is speaking up for his own sake in a manner that is certain and clear.

Ollie finds his voice and talks to Bob

When Ollie begins to find his voice, it is quite possible that Bob might respond in the following ways:

- **Diverting the topic.** Diverting the topic or turning the topic back onto Ollie is a tactic that Bob may use to take the focus away from himself.

- **Be more insulting**. Bob might react to Ollie's request by adding another insult. This is when Ollie needs to keep his line between them solid and strong.

- **Change back.** Bob may try to get Ollie to change back to their old tease/react/tease/react pattern by trying harder to draw Ollie into the Bully-game. Things might get worse before they get better. *Be prepared for what the other person might do.*

Now it's your turn

Imagine yourself speaking up to the person who has been bullying you. Imagine telling them that you want them to stop teasing you.

> **Most importantly, stay safe. Don't say or do anything that might put you at risk.**

Write a list of what you would like to say.

STRATEGY FIVE:

Engage Support

Ollie seeks help and support

If you are getting upset by the teasing comments and bullying behaviour of others, then you may need some help and support.

Support:

- shows you that you are not alone
- can help you to see your situation differently
- can be from your parents, youth leader, your school's wellbeing coordinator, from a professional counsellor or a trusted adult or friend.

There are several reasons why you might be reluctant to ask for help.

Courage: Telling another person of an incident or series of incidents of bullying and teasing can take courage. You might feel that it is wrong or weak to have to admit that you cannot handle this on your own. You might be worried about disappointing your parents or fear that you are broken in some way or that you are being pathetic.

Sometimes, parents can be the last people to learn that their child has been bullied. Please know that seeking help does not mean that you are pathetic, or broken, or weak. Seeking help is one of the most courageous things you can do.

You may not want them to intervene. You will need to discuss whether or not you need someone to intervene. If there has been physical bullying, then help is necessary. Your safety and wellbeing are most important. I know that many young people do not want their parents involved in fear of it making matters worse, but that is the Bully-game in full swing. Do you think you are at risk? Do you feel in danger? *This is a conversation that has to be had*.

You may be worried about being a burden. Life is full of problems, and you may not want to add to the long list that already exists. Do not let this be a reason for not seeking help.

You may think that this is your fault. Insulting words from others can be a double-whammy. Not only has someone said something cruel to you, but you may also believe that you deserved it somehow. **IT IS NOT YOUR FAULT!** It is not your fault if another person is mean to you – they are caught in the Bully-game too. You are not responsible for what another person may do.

Take a deep breath and reach out for help.

Now it's your turn

Can you make a list of people you could turn to for help?

CHAPTER EIGHT:

Wrapping it up

Ollie knows the strategies for his New-game

Now that Ollie is no longer playing the Bully-game, he is no longer at the mercy of Bob's behaviour. His New-game, and idea of himself, are helped by his new strategies that prevent Bob from **G**aining **A**ccess to his **M**ind and **E**motions. The New-game strategies for **Bully Resilience** work together to help Ollie make the choices that have always been there. *Are you ready to try your own New-game?*

Be a team

Come up with a plan of action. Imagine potential scenarios and practice your responses with another person. There will be days when it works, and days when you slip back into the old Bully-game.

There may also be days when it all gets too much, but don't beat yourself up, you can try again next time. It might mean that while you learn the New-game at school you need extra support from others. You may need to talk about it more when you get home.

Choosing to respond differently takes practice because you are learning a new **process**. You are actually learning a new skill. I still get caught out from time to time. It is quite easy to slip into playing the Bully-game when an unsuspecting and attacking remark is followed by another and then another. Once I recognise the Bully-game, I begin using my strategies.

Remember the ABC Behaviour Burger

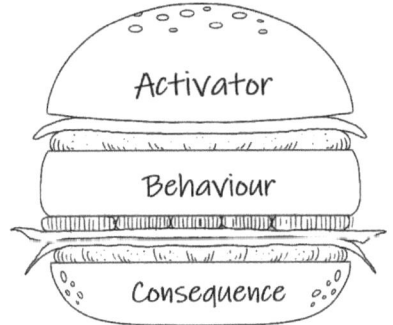

Once you learn about the ABC Behaviour Burger, you might even begin to see it. Think about what it is that you may be reacting to. What was in place before the tease and what happened after? Why is it that some insults hurt more than others? By working out these things about yourself, you will understand yourself better. If it is causing problems for you, then you might need to talk to somebody about it.

Just because someone says something bad to you, does not mean you have to respond. A question that is always worth asking is *will it be helpful?*

The journey to resilience is on-going

There are days when we can do it, and days when we just can't seem to. Despite resilience being within us, there are some days when it seems difficult to access. It takes practice. You can now play the New-game, in this game you protect yourself and you do not allow another to **G**ain **A**ccess to your **M**ind and **E**motions. Stop playing the Bully-game and change the game. Start to play your own New-game, where you are in control and you are the main player.

It is time to be Bully Resilient by Changing the Game.

BULLY RESILIENCE:

Changing the Game

For more information visit

www.bullyresilience.com.au

BIBLIOGRAPHY

Aron EN. **The highly sensitive person; how to thrive when the world overwhelms you**, Harmony books, New York, 1996.

Aron EN. **Psychotherapy and the highly sensitive person**, Routledge Taylor & Francis Group, New York, 2010.

Brown B. **Rising strong**, Penguin Random House, London, 2015.

Edleman S, Remond L. Good Thinking: **A teenagers' guide to managing stress and emotions using CBT**, HarperCollins Publishers, Sydney, 2017.

Field EM. **Bully busting; how to help your children deal with teasing and bullying**, Finch Publishing, Sydney, 1999.

Ginsburg KR, Jablow MM. **Building resilience in children and teens (third ed); giving kids roots and wings**, American Academy of Pediatrics, Elk Grove Village, 2015.

Harris R. **ACT made simple**, New Harbinger Publications, Oakland, 2009.

Harris R. **The confidence gap; from fear to freedom**, Penguin Random House, Australia, 2010.

Hayes SC, Strosahl KD, Wilson KG. **Acceptance and Commitment Therapy; the process and practice of mindful change**, The Guilford Press, New York, 2012.

Joseph S. Authentic: **How to be yourself and why it matters**, Little, Brown Book Group, London, 2017.

Lerner H. **The dance of anger; a woman's guide to changing the patterns of intimate relationships**, Harper Collins, Australia, 2014.

Seligman M. **The optimistic child**, William Heinemann, Sydney, 1995.

Wiseman R. **Queen bees & wannabes; helping your daughter survive cliques, gossip, boyfriends & other realities of adolescence**, Piatkus Books Limited, London, 2002.

www.ingramcontent.com/pod-product-compliance
Lightning Source LLC
Chambersburg PA
CBHW062105290426
44110CB00022B/2720